KINGFISHER
READERS

level

GW01003700

The Environment

Deborah Chancellor

KINGFISHER

First published 2013 by Kingfisher
an imprint of Macmillan Children's Books
20 New Wharf Road, London N1 9RR
Associated companies throughout the world
www.panmacmillan.com

Series editor: Polly Goodman
Literacy consultant: Hilary Horton

ISBN: 978-0-7534-3101-6
Copyright © Macmillan Publishers International Ltd 2013

9 8 7 6 5 4 3 2

2TR/0815/WKT/UG/105MA
A CIP catalogue record for this book is available from the British Library.
Printed in China

Picture credits

The Publisher would like to thank the following for permission to reproduce their material. Every care has
been taken to trace copyright holders. However, if there have been unintentional omissions or failure to trace
copyright holders, we apologize and will, if informed, endeavour to make corrections in any future edition.
Top = t; Bottom = b; Centre = c; Left = l; Right = r
Cover Corbis/Reuters; cover t KF Archive; Cover c Shutterstock (SS)/Juriah Mosin; Cover b Corbis/
Radius; 2l Corbis/Reuters; 2lc Corbis/Ocean; 2c Corbis/Joel Sartore/NGS; 2cr Corbis/Radius; 2r Alamy/
Gary Crabbe; 3l Corbis/Radius; 3cl Alamy/Ariadne Van Zandbergen; 3c SS/Matt Jones; 3cr KF Archive
(KF); 3r Photoshot/Xinhua News Agency; 4l SS/beata becia; 4–5 KF; 6 SS/Anton Foltin; 7 KF; 8 SS/Juriah
Mosin; 9 Corbis/Radius; 10 SS/Antonio S.; 11 Corbis/Ocean; 12 KF; 13t Corbis/DLILL; 13b Corbis/Radius;
14 SS/Loskutnikov; 15 SS/fotohunter; 16 Corbis/Ocean; 17tl KF; 17b SS/achios; 18cl Corbis/Peter
Andrews/Reuters; 18bl SS Fedor Korolevsky; 18br SS Danii Balashov; 19 KF; 20 SS/Ian Bracegirdle;
21 SS/Dmitry Berkut or /pzRomashka; 22tl Photoshot/NHPA; 22b SS/Rafael Ramiraz Lee; 23 Corbis/
STR/Reuters; 24 Getty/BAL; 25t Corbis/DLILL; 25b Getty/Science Faction Jewels; 26 Alamy/Steve
Morgan; 27t Corbis/Julie Dermansky; 27b Corbis/Joel Sartore/NGS; 28 Corbis/Reuters; 29t Getty/Flickr;
29b Corbis/David Frazier; 30 Photoshot/Xinhua News Agency; 31 SS/Volodynyr Golnyk; 33t SS/Caitlin
Mirra; 33b Alamy/Ariadne Van Zandbergen; 34tr Corbis/Pete Oxford; 35 Alamy/Gary Crabbe; 36 KF; 37
SS/Eric Gevaert; 38 Shutterstock/Otmar Smit; 39t Photoshot; 39b KF; 40 SS/Matt Jones; 41 SS/Dmitry
Naumov; 42 Alamy/Jenny Matthews; 43 Corbis/Surf; 44 Getty/Lifesize; 45t Getty/First Life; 45b SS/Valery
Kraynov; 45b SS/Quang Ho; 45b SS/TigerForce; 46l Corbis/Reuters; 46lc Corbis/
Ocean; 46c Corbis/Joel Sartore/NGS; 46cr Corbis/Radius; 46r Alamy/Gary Crabbe; 47l Corbis/Radius;
47cl Alamy/Ariadne Van Zandbergen; 47c SS/Matt Jones; 47cr KF; 47r Photoshot/Xinhua News Agency

Contents

Wonderful world

We use the word environment in many different ways. When we talk about the environment, we may just mean our immediate surroundings, and everything around us that we can see, smell, taste, touch and hear.

The environment is all around us.

Howler monkey

Blue morpho butterfly

The word environment can mean something much bigger than this. It can mean all the things that we need to stay alive. That means the land we live on, the air we breathe, the food we eat and the water we drink. It can even mean the whole of the natural world.

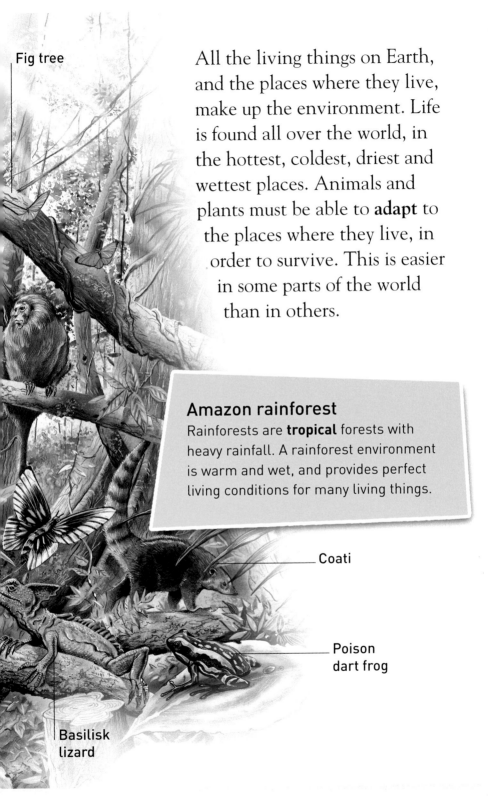

Fig tree

All the living things on Earth, and the places where they live, make up the environment. Life is found all over the world, in the hottest, coldest, driest and wettest places. Animals and plants must be able to **adapt** to the places where they live, in order to survive. This is easier in some parts of the world than in others.

Amazon rainforest
Rainforests are **tropical** forests with heavy rainfall. A rainforest environment is warm and wet, and provides perfect living conditions for many living things.

Coati

Poison dart frog

Basilisk lizard

Life on Earth

There is an amazing variety of life on Earth. This variety is called biodiversity, and it is an important feature of the natural environment. Some places have more **species** (types) of animals, plants, **bacteria** and **fungi** than others, which means they have greater biodiversity. For example, two thirds of the world's plant species are found in tropical rainforests.

It is a different story in the Arctic and Antarctic. There are fewer living things in **polar lands**, because it is hard to survive the extreme conditions. In Antarctica, no **mammals** live on the land. No trees grow there either, because it is the coldest and windiest place on Earth.

The Sonoran **desert**, in North America, is an area of high biodiversity. Many plant species grow there.

Every animal on Earth can be sorted into a group, depending on how it is described. There are six main groups of animal species:

ladybird

goldfish

Invertebrates: animals without backbones, such as insects, spiders, worms and many more

Fish: scaly animals that live only in water, lay eggs and breathe through gills.

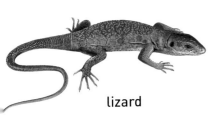
lizard

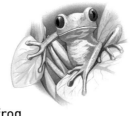
tree frog

Reptiles: animals with scaly skin that live in land or in water, such as lizards, crocodiles, turtles and snakes

Amphibians: animals that live partly in water and partly on land, such as frogs, toads and newts

sparrow

panda

Birds: animals that have wings, feathers and beaks, and lay eggs

Mammals: animals that have fur or hair, and feed their young on milk made in the mother's body

Amazing places

The place where an animal lives is called a habitat. Lots of species can share the same habitat; for example, a pond may contain many different fish, amphibians, insects and plants. These living things all depend on their particular habitat for food and shelter. If their habitat is destroyed, animals can find it difficult or impossible to survive. The world's habitats include deserts, grasslands and forests.

Rainforests provide a habitat for thousands of different species. These parrots are roosting on a fig tree in the Amazon rainforest.

Oceans cover more than two thirds of the Earth's surface, and are home to over a quarter of a million species of animals and plants. There are many different ocean habitats, such as **kelp forests** and **coral reefs**. Each ocean habitat shelters a different variety of species. In warm tropical oceans, many kinds of fish, turtle, octopus and sea snake live among coral reefs. These creatures are often brightly coloured, so they are hard to spot near the coral.

These corals are near the north coast of West Papua, in Indonesia. More than 1,100 species of fish are found on the coral reef in this part of the world.

Underwater habitat

A coral reef looks like a colourful garden, but it does not contain any plants. Each type of coral is actually a colony of billions of tiny invertebrates, called polyps.

Living together

Animals and plants need food, water and shelter. This means they have to live in groups, sharing the same habitat and depending on each other to survive. A group of animals and plants that live together in a habitat like this is called an **ecosystem**. The environment is made up of many different ecosystems, some small and others much bigger.

Ecosystems can be huge; for example, a whole forest is an ecosystem. Birds, insects, mammals and plants all shelter in a forest and rely on each other for food. But the same forest may contain many smaller ecosystems. An oak tree can be an ecosystem all by itself, supporting a group of small creatures and plant species that share the same habitat and depend on each other.

This squirrel is eating an acorn – the animal and the nut both belong to the same ecosystem.

A lion hunts a zebra in the grasslands.

The grasslands of Africa have some amazing wildlife, and many different ecosystems. For example, lions, zebra and grass are part of the same ecosystem. Packs of lions hunt herds of zebra, which feed on the grass. The lions, zebra and grass all need to exist together in the ecosystem to keep it working.

An oak tree is an ecosystem for many plants and animals.

Branches and leaves: support insects such as bees and moths, birds such as sparrows and hawks, and climbing mammals such as squirrels

Trunk: supports insects

Roots and leaf litter: support bacteria, earthworms, fungi and woodlice

Earth's climates

The pattern of weather you get in a place over a long period of time is called its climate. Climates vary around the world. However, different parts of the world have similar climates that provide habitats for similar plants and animals. These areas of similar climates are called biomes and they are usually made up of several habitats. Some smaller biomes are unusual, because they consist of just one habitat. For example, Arctic tundra is both a habitat and a biome.

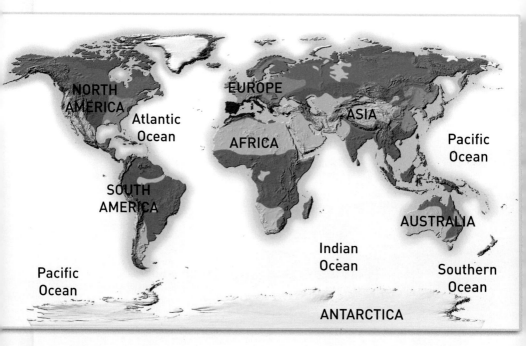

You can find the same type of biome in different parts of the Earth.

In the Sonoran desert, USA, the large cardon cactus can store more than a tonne of water in its stem to help it survive the hot, dry climate.

It is hard for living things to survive in extreme climates, but animals and plants find clever ways of adapting to the conditions where they live. For example, in the Arctic, fox cubs keep warm in snowy dens. In deserts, cactus plants store water in their stems.

KEY
Polar
Arctic tundra
Mountains
Coniferous forests
Temperate forests
Tropical forests
Shrublands
Grasslands
Deserts
Wetlands
Coral reefs

In winter, the Arctic fox has an extra layer of fat and a thick fur coat to help it survive the icy cold.

Planet Earth

The Earth is a planet in space. When we look at photos of our planet, we can see the oceans, the **continents** and the swirling clouds in the **atmosphere**.

From space, the Earth looks blue, because more than two thirds of it is covered with water.

The atmosphere is a layer of gases that protects planet Earth, absorbing harmful rays from the Sun and balancing the temperature. Gases in the atmosphere include nitrogen, **oxygen** and **carbon dioxide**. There could be no life on Earth without the atmosphere.

All green plants take in **energy** from the Sun, water and **minerals** from the soil and carbon dioxide from the air. They then give off water and oxygen into the atmosphere. If too many trees and green plants are cut down, levels of carbon dioxide will rise, disturbing the fine balance of the Earth's atmosphere.

Green plants help to balance the different gases in the atmosphere.

Weather and seasons

Weather forms in the lowest part of the atmosphere, up to ten kilometres above the ground, within a layer of the atmosphere called the troposphere. Rain and snow form in clouds, and the movement of air in the atmosphere creates winds. The Sun's rays travel through the atmosphere to warm the Earth and give us hot, sunny weather.

In parts of the world with four seasons, there is a regular pattern of weather. Summer is hot and sunny, autumn is cool and windy, winter can be cold and snowy, and spring brings sunshine and showers.

Exosphere
(10,000km)

Thermosphere
(690km)

Mesosphere
(85km)

Stratosphere
(50km)

Troposphere
(0–15km)

There are five main layers in the Earth's atmosphere.

In summer, the Sun shines for longer and flowers bloom.

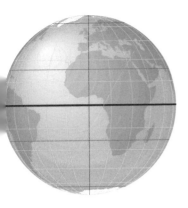

On a map, the Equator is shown as a line around the Earth. The areas around the Equator are the hottest on the planet.

The Equator is an imaginary line that runs around the middle of the Earth. In parts of the world near the Equator, it is very hot all year round. These parts are called the tropics. There are only two seasons in tropical places – we call them wet and dry seasons. The wet season is also known as the **monsoon** season.

In tropical countries, heavy monsoon rains can cause floods.

The Earth's riches

Things from nature that are useful to people are called natural resources. The Earth is rich in natural resources, such as metals and **fossil fuels**. They may be found under the ground or under the sea bed. For example, aluminium and iron are metals that are found in mines underground.

The coal in this mine is hundreds of metres under the ground.

Gold is a precious metal that is sometimes used to make valuable coins.

Wood is a common material that is used to make practical things, like this bowl.

Fossil fuels are made from the decayed remains of dead plants and animals. They take hundreds of millions of years to form, deep under the ground. Oil, gas and coal are different kinds of fossil fuels. Oil rigs drill under the surface of the Earth to collect oil. Some oil rigs are on land, and others are at sea.

We burn fossil fuels to provide energy for transport, homes and places of work. We are using them up so quickly that some scientists predict coal may only last another few hundred years, and all our natural gas and oil may run out in less than a hundred years.

Oil rigs drill for oil deep under the sea bed.

Environment in danger

In some places, air pollution is so bad that people wear face masks so that they can try to avoid breathing in the pollution.

The environment faces many difficult problems and dangers. For example, we rely on natural resources, such as coal, oil and gas, but we know they will not last forever. We are overusing the Earth's precious resources and upsetting the natural balance of the environment.

Pollution is harming many places on Earth. Pollution is any kind of dirt or waste that damages the environment. Toxic **chemicals** from factories and power stations are making the land, sea and air less healthy and safe. Important habitats are being harmed, putting many rare species and fragile ecosystems in danger.

Some factories create smoke that contains harmful chemicals that pollute the air we breathe.

Scientists warn that temperatures around the world are rising faster than ever before. This is **global warming**, and it is happening because humans are putting large amounts of harmful gases into the Earth's atmosphere. These gases are trapping too much of the Sun's warmth in the Earth's atmosphere. As a result, the world is slowly getting warmer.

The carbon cycle
Gases that help cause global warming are called greenhouse gases. One of the most important greenhouse gases is carbon dioxide. This gas is made when animals breathe and any materials made from carbon are burnt, such as fossil fuels.

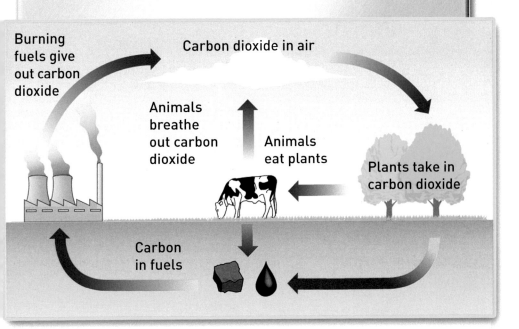

Burning fuels give out carbon dioxide

Carbon dioxide in air

Animals breathe out carbon dioxide

Animals eat plants

Plants take in carbon dioxide

Carbon in fuels

Disappearing habitats

Many habitats around the world are at risk. Every day, fragile habitats such as rainforests are destroyed to make way for cattle farms, mines and other **industries**.

Some species of animals are put in danger, because their habitats are disappearing. Rare animals may even die out altogether, because they can't adapt quickly enough to survive in new habitats.

In the last 50 years, more than half of the world's rainforests have been destroyed.

There are more than seven billion people on the planet, and this number is getting bigger all the time. It is hard to protect all animal habitats, when so many humans need space to live and food to eat.

The growing world population is a threat to animal habitats.

These corals in the Caribbean have died as a result of global warming.

Pollution is a big problem for many habitats. For example, air pollution can mix with clouds, making acid rain fall. Over time, acid rain can kill trees and destroy large areas of forest.

Another danger for precious habitats is global warming. This is caused by humans putting high levels of harmful gases in the atmosphere. Some coral reefs are dying because the oceans are getting warmer. Warmer water kills **algae** that live on the corals, and the corals do not have enough food to survive. Sadly, when the reefs die, so do all the animals and plants that live on them.

Animals at risk

When the last of a species dies out, we say that it becomes **extinct**. Over the past hundred years, more species have become extinct than ever before. Some experts believe it will take only another hundred years for up to half of all the species on Earth to disappear.

Today, many animal species are in danger of becoming extinct. This is often because they are losing their natural habitat. For example, there are only about 30,000 orang-utans left in the wild, and a third of all amphibian species are now **endangered**.

The last quagga
A quagga was a kind of zebra that lived in southern Africa. It was hunted to extinction for its meat and leather. The last quagga died in a zoo in Amsterdam, the Netherlands, in 1883.

Orang-utans live in the rainforest. Their forest habitat is being cut down for timber and to make way for palm oil plantations.

Pollution is a threat to many animals. Rubbish in the sea is a hazard for endangered marine species such as the leatherback turtle. Many turtles have died after swallowing plastic bags, balloons or other floating plastic waste.

Turtles can mistake plastic bags for jellyfish, and die after eating them.

Disasters caused by people

Disasters can happen when there are industrial accidents, such as when chemicals leak from a factory, or when oil spills into the sea. Animals are poisoned by pollution and whole ecosystems are destroyed. Local communities and industries are also badly affected.

Long-term disaster
In 1986, there was an accident at a **nuclear power** station at Chernobyl, in Ukraine, and 323,749 square kilometres of land were **contaminated**. Many thousands of people died or became ill, and children born in the area have had serious health problems. The land around Chernobyl is still contaminated, and people and animals cannot live there safely.

These scientists are checking the levels of radiation on the land at Chernobyl, 20 years after the accident happened.

After the oil spill, there was a huge clean-up operation in the Gulf of Mexico. These boats pulled nets across the sea water to skim off some of the oil.

In May 2010, there was an explosion on an oil rig in the Gulf of Mexico. As a result, hundreds of millions of litres of oil gushed into the sea. Many sea animals were killed in the Gulf, and coastal industries ground to a halt. People called it the worst environmental disaster in US history.

Sea birds can drown if their feathers are soaked in oil. People have to clean off the oil for them.

Pollution problems

Worldwide, factories and transport create huge amounts of pollution. Every minute of every day, factories and farms leak **toxic** waste into the soil and into the water supply. Harmful gases are released into the air when materials are burned in power stations and factories.

Most of the plastic bags we use end up in landfill sites. They take hundreds of years to rot.

A lot of our rubbish is taken to landfill sites, where it is crushed by bulldozers and buried in big holes in the ground. Poisonous chemicals may seep into the earth, and greenhouse gases such as methane may rise up into the atmosphere.

Smog city
Traffic fumes and industrial pollution make clouds of smog over big cities. Smog is a mixture of natural fog and smoke created by traffic and factories.

Sometimes, waste from sewage plants, where waste water is treated to get rid of harmful materials, leaks into nearby rivers. For example, in 2011 in central China, a big sewage spill had terrible effects on the environment. In just three days, thousands of fish were killed in polluted rivers in Hubei Province.

This man is collecting dead fish from a polluted pond near the city of Wuhan, China.

Climate change

Different parts of the world have different climates. There is **evidence** that these climates are changing because of global warming. Scientists do not know exactly how much warmer the Earth will get, or how quickly this may happen. Many predict that temperatures will rise by 2°C by 2050.

This may not sound much, but if it happens, it will be very bad news for the environment. Some parts of the world may turn into desert, causing food and water shortages for millions of people. In India, much less rice and wheat may be produced. Global warming could change our weather patterns, including the amount of rain or snow that falls in different places. Storms may become more common in some parts of the world.

In the future, **famine** and **drought** could become more common.

In the future, polar lands such as the Arctic and Antarctic may become warmer, and rising temperatures could make the ice melt at the polar regions. This would make sea levels rise all over the world, flooding many coastal towns and cities. The results of this would be devastating.

The big melt
Polar ice is already melting faster than ever before because of global warming. This affects polar wildlife. For example, when Arctic glaciers melt away, polar bears find it very hard to survive.

This massive iceberg was formed when it broke away from an ice sheet in the Antarctic.

Wild weather

In many parts of the world there are extreme forms of weather. For example, in polar lands, there are freezing blizzards, and in tropical countries, there are huge storms called hurricanes, typhones or cyclones. Changing climate patterns are making weather more extreme in some places. Tropical storms seem to be getting stronger and more dangerous.

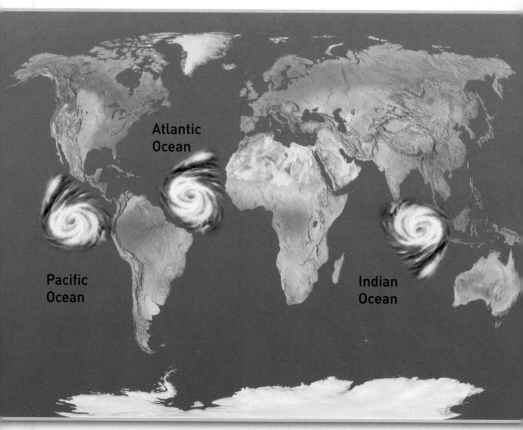

Atlantic
Ocean

Pacific
Ocean

Indian
Ocean

This map shows where tropical storms happen: cyclones in the Pacific Ocean, hurricanes in the Atlantic Ocean and typhoons in Southeast Asia.

Are hurricanes getting worse?
In August 2005, Hurricane Katrina swept through the US city of New Orleans, causing serious floods. The hurricane destroyed about 275,000 homes, ten times more than any other **natural disaster** in US history. Was Hurricane Katrina caused by climate change? There is no way to know for sure, but we do know that powerful hurricanes like this are likely to happen more often as a result of climate change.

Global warming makes droughts happen more often. If no rain falls or a place gets much less rain than usual, there is a drought. This means there is not enough water and crops fail. People die because they do not have enough to eat or drink.

People can't survive for very long without water. This boy in Cambodia collects water from a water pump in his village.

33

Conservation challenge

There are many things people can do to cut pollution, clean up the environment and save endangered species. For example, we know that when habitats are destroyed, animals are put at risk. We can try to stop this from happening. This kind of work is called conservation.

Conservation projects can turn fragile habitats into national parks and wildlife reserves. In these protected zones, the land is carefully looked after, hunting is banned and the animals are kept safe.

This rare mountain gorilla lives in a national park in Uganda, in Africa.

Rainforests have been growing for more than 400 million years. They are called the 'lungs' of the planet, because they take in carbon dioxide from the atmosphere and let out oxygen. Many people are fighting to protect rainforests.

These conservation workers are putting an electronic tag on a harpy eagle in the Amazon rainforest.

Understanding conservation

People need to learn about the environment, to understand why it must be protected. National parks and wildlife reserves run education programmes, to teach children and adults about conservation. The money that tourists pay to visit is used to help look after endangered species and habitats.

Animal rescue

Conservation groups are working hard to save endangered animals. For example, many charities have set up projects to protect animals that are in danger of becoming extinct. You can support this work by giving money – for example, you can pay to 'adopt' a rare animal, such as a polar bear or tiger.

This map shows where some important conservation work is taking place around the world.

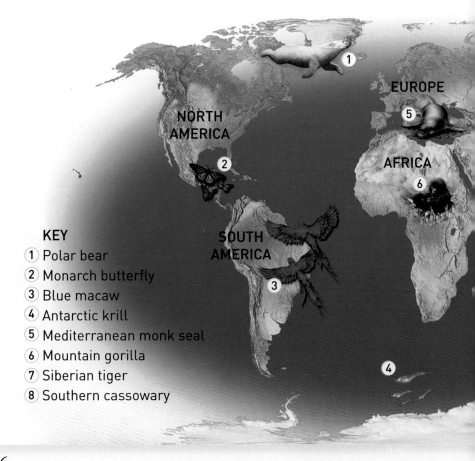

EUROPE

NORTH
AMERICA

AFRICA

SOUTH
AMERICA

KEY
1. Polar bear
2. Monarch butterfly
3. Blue macaw
4. Antarctic krill
5. Mediterranean monk seal
6. Mountain gorilla
7. Siberian tiger
8. Southern cassowary

When an animal is endangered, it means that there are not many of its kind left. Endangered animals must be encouraged to have babies, so the population of that species can begin to grow.

Sometimes, breeding programmes are very successful. In the Amazon rainforest, a monkey called the golden lion tamarin was very nearly extinct. In the 1970s, there were fewer than 200 golden lion tamarins in the wild. A conservation programme prevented this animal from dying out. Now, there are more than a thousand in the wild, and the numbers are rising.

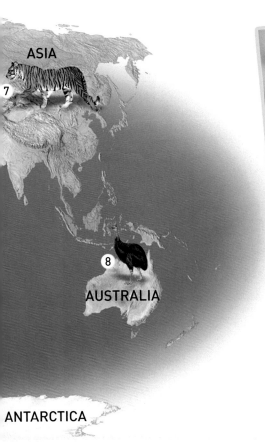

Much of the golden lion tamarin's forest habitat has been destroyed, but these monkeys have been saved from extinction due to work by conservation groups.

Clean power

Some ways of producing energy make far less pollution than fossil fuels. For example, solar power turns the Sun's rays into electricity. It is clean to produce and the Sun's rays will not run out. A huge solar power station has been built in Spain, for example. It produces electricity for 180,000 homes in the city of Seville.

Solar panels on rooftops can provide power for our homes.

Wind turns the long blades of wind turbines, producing large amounts of electricity for towns and cities. Out at sea, wave power can also be used to make electricity.

In a wind farm, many turbines work together to generate electricity.

The Three Gorges Dam is the world's largest electricity plant.

The power of flowing water can be used to make electricity. This is called hydro-electric power. Dams are built across rivers to create hydro-electric power. The biggest dam in the world is the Three Gorges Dam in China. It generates as much energy as 18 coal power stations, without causing air pollution. In spite of this, many people are unhappy about the Three Gorges Dam. Cities, towns and villages were flooded to make way for it, and more than a million people were forced to move home.

Saving energy

We can help the environment by saving energy. If we use less electricity and fuel, we will not have to produce so much of it in the first place. There are lots of things we can do to save energy. For example, in winter we can wear warmer clothes instead of turning up the heating. We can also try to stop heat escaping from our homes. Remember to shut the doors and windows!

Switch off
Always switch off the light when you leave a room. Don't leave your TV, computer or other electrical gadgets on standby, because this uses nearly as much energy as when they are fully on.

Riding a bike is good
for the environment
and keeps you fit, too.

There are more than 600 million cars in the world,
and many of them make unnecessary journeys. Think
of different ways of travelling, such as walking, cycling
or using public transport. Buses, trains and trams carry
lots of people, so they don't use up as much fuel per
person as cars do.

Waste watch

We don't just waste energy – we also waste huge amounts of food. Every year, about 35 million tonnes of food is thrown away in the USA. Much of this food is not even touched or opened before it ends up in the bin. We can easily cut back on how much food we waste, if we only buy what we really need.

Food waste

Supermarkets sell food in big bags and containers. This leads to waste, as we can't always eat all the food we buy before it goes off. Write a shopping list to stop you buying things you don't need, and haven't got room to store.

Volunteers show they can make a good meal using rejected food. Supermarkets throw away huge amounts of fruit and vegetables, because they do not look perfect.

In some parts of the world, there is not enough water to go round. In places where there is more water, it is often wasted. As climate change affects the amount of rain that falls around the world, we will need to be much more careful about water in the future.

Turn it off!
Turn off the tap when you brush your teeth. This saves a lot of water every day.

Reuse and recycle

Making things in factories uses up energy and natural resources, and creates pollution. The more we throw away, the more new goods have to be made to replace them. It is much better for the environment if we reuse things. This means fewer new things need to be made, and there is not so much waste and pollution.

If you can't reuse something yourself, give it away or sell it, so that someone else can reuse it instead.

You can pick up a bargain at a second-hand sale, and help protect the environment at the same time.

When something old and unwanted is **recycled**, it is made into something new and useful. Recycling is good for the environment, because it saves the energy and natural resources that are needed to make new materials.

This fleece was made from about 20 recycled plastic bottles.

Take extra care with your rubbish. Before you throw it away, sort it out to be recycled. Always put glass, paper, cardboard, steel, aluminium and plastic bottles in the recycling bin. Don't mix them up with materials that can't be recycled, such as hard plastic and polystyrene.

Remember – our environment is amazing. We must all do our bit to keep it that way!

Do recycle:
- glass and plastic bottles
- paper and cardboard
- steel and aluminium cans

Glossary

adapt To change in order to survive in new conditions.

algae Very tiny, plant-like living things that live in water.

atmosphere The layer of gases around the Earth.

bacteria Very tiny living things.

carbon dioxide One of the greenhouse gases in the atmosphere that cause global warming.

chemical Another word for a substance.

contaminated Containing harmful, unhealthy substances.

continent One of the seven large land masses in the world.

coral reef An underwater structure made from tiny sea animals, called polyps.

desert An area of very dry land.

drought A long period without rain.

ecosystem A group of living things that share a habitat and depend on each other.

endangered In danger of dying out.

energy The power to do things, or make things work.

evidence Proof of something.

extinct When an animal or plant species dies out completely.

famine A terrible shortage of food.

fossil fuel A source of energy that is buried deep under the ground, such as gas, oil and coal.

fungi (singular: fungus) A group of living things, including mushrooms and toadstools, that are not plants or animals.

global warming The rise in the overall temperature of the Earth's atmosphere.

industry A business that makes and sells things.

kelp forest An area in the ocean where lots of kelp (a type of seaweed) grows.

mammal An animal with fur or hair that drinks its mother's milk when it is young.

mineral A natural material that is part of rocks and soil.

monsoon A wind that brings heavy rain and floods to India and Southeast Asia.

natural disaster A natural event that brings great destruction, for example a volcanic eruption, earthquake, tsunami, storm, flood or wildfire.

nuclear power Energy that is produced from a controlled nuclear reaction in a power station.

oxygen One of the gases in the air. We breathe it to stay alive.

polar lands The areas around the north and south poles.

pollution Harmful chemicals that make a place or thing dirty or poison it.

recycle To convert waste materials into new materials.

species A group of plants or animals that breed together to produce young.

toxic Poisonous.

tropical From a hot, wet part of the world near the Equator.

Index